Richard J.S. Stevens

Sacred Music

Consisting of Selections From the Great English and Italian masters, Handel, Purcel,

Green, Croft, Marcello, Steffani, Pergolese

Richard J.S. Stevens

Sacred Music
Consisting of Selections From the Great English and Italian masters, Handel, Purcel, Green,
Croft, Marcello, Steffani, Pergolese

ISBN/EAN: 9783337127640

Printed in Europe, USA, Canada, Australia, Japan

Cover: Foto ©Thomas Meinert / pixelio.de

More available books at **www.hansebooks.com**

Sacred Music

Dedicated to his Grace

The ARCHBISHOP of CANTERBURY

Consisting of

Selections from the great English & Italian

MASTERS

Handel, Purcel, Green, Croft

MARCELLO, STEFFANI, PERGOLESE &c

the whole

Selected, Adapted & Arranged for

One Two Three or Four Voices

and the

Piano Forte or Organ

By

R. I. S. STEVENS.

Organist of the Charterhouse & Temple, Gresham Professor &c.

in 3 Vol.^s

Vol. 1.
Pr. 1. 1. 0.

London, Printed & Sold by PRESTON, at his Wholesale Warehouses 97, Strand.

To His Grace

The Archbishop of Canterbury.

The following Publication

intended to facilitate and promote

the Performance of Sacred Music

in private Families, is by permission

gratefully inscribed,

by His Grace's

most obliged

and obedient

humble Servant,

Richard John Samuel Stevens.

INDEX to VOLUME I.

TRIO.

For two Sopranos and a Bass.

Psalm 33rd.   Steffani.

Moderato

Re-joice in the Lord O ye

Re -

Tasto Solo

- - joice in the Lord O ye Righteous Re-joice O ye Righteous Rejoice in the

Righteous ye Righteous Re-joice in the Lord O ye Righteous Rejoice in the

Engrav'd by TStraight · N?7. Lambeth Walk, Surry.

for.
Rejoice in the Lord O ye Righteous ye
tr.
Lord O ye Righ - - - teous Rejoice in the Lord O ye Righteous ye
Lord O ye Righ - - - teous Rejoice in the
pia.
Righteous Re_joice in the Lord O ye Righ - - teous Re_joice in the
pia.
Righteous Re_joice - - - - - O ye Righ - - teous Re_joice in the
pia.
Lord O ye Righteous Re_joice O ye Righ - - teous Re_joice in the
pia.
for.
Lord Re_joice in the Lord O ye Righteous Re_joice Re_joice in the
for.
Lord Rejoice in the Lord O ye Righteous Re_joice Re_
for.
Lord O ye Righteous Re_joice ye Righteous Rejoice in the Lord O ye
for.

Lord   Rejoice O Rejoice in the Lord

_joice in the Lord O ye Righteous Rejoice in the Lord Rejoice in the

Righteous Re_joice in the Lord Rejoice in the Lord   Re_

8 7   6   5 9 8 7 6 5   8 7
      7 6 5 4 3

pia.

Re_joice O Re_joice in the Lord   **·S.** *Organ*   *for.*

Lord O ye Righteous Re_joice in the Lord   **·S.**

joice in the Lord Rejoice in the Lord   **·S.**

6   6 5 9 8 7 6. 5   **·S.**   *for.*
    7 6 5 4 3

for.

For

6   6   3 6   5   6 5   *for.*
                              4 4
                                 3

it beco_meth well the Juſt to be thankful be__co_ _meth well the
for.
For it becometh well the Juſt to be _ thankful be _ co_ _ _meth
pia.
For it beco__meth well the Juſt to be
tr
pia.
Juſt _ _ _ _ to be thank _ _ _ ful Re _ _ joice _ _ _ _ re _
pia.
well the Juſt to be thank _ _ _ ful For it beco _ meth well the
pia.
tr
for.
thankful be_ _co_ _meth well the Juſt to be thank_ _ _ ful Re_
joice it be_ _co_ _meth well the Juſt to be_ _ thank_ _ful
Juſt to be thankful be_ cometh the Juſt to be thank _ _ _ ful for
for.

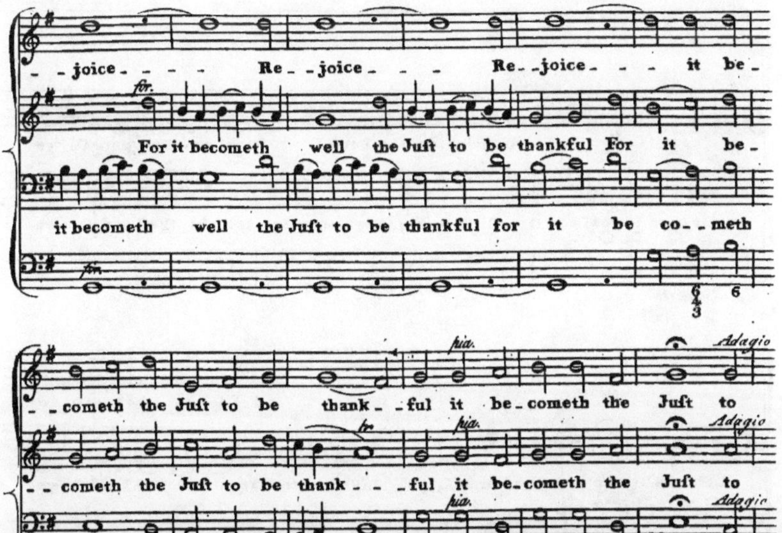
joice Re joice Re joice it be
for.
For it becometh well the Just to be thankful For it be
it becometh well the Just to be thankful for it be co meth
for.
pia.
Adagio
cometh the Just to be thank ful it be cometh the Just to
tr.
pia.
Adagio
cometh the Just to be thank ful it be cometh the Just to
pia.
Adagio
well the Just to be thank ful it be cometh the Just to
pia.
Adagio
Organ pia
tempo
be thank ful.
tr.
be thank ful.
be thank ful.
tempo
pia.

for.
- - joice in the Lord Re-joice in the Lord O ye Righteous Re- - joice Re-
- - joice in the Lord ye Righteous Re-joice in the Lord O ye Righ-teous
for.
- - joice in the Lord O ye Righteous Re- - joice Re- - joice Re-joice in the
for.
for.
- - joice in the Lord Re-joice O Re-joice in the Lord
for.
pia.
Re-joice in the Lord O ye Righteous Re-joice in the Lord Re-
Lord O ye Righteous Re-joice in the Lord Re-joice in the Lord
pia.
tr.
Organ
for.
Re-joice O Re-joice in the Lord.
tr.
- - joice in the Lord O ye righteous Re-joice in the Lord.
pia.
Re-joice in the Lord Re-joice in the Lord.
pia.
tr.

ANTHEM.

From the Burial Service, For Four Voices.   Purcell.

Grave.

Soprano.

Thou knowest Lord the se_crets of our Hearts Shut not

Alto. an Octave lower.

Thou knowest Lord the se_crets of our Hearts Shut not

Tenor. An Octave lower.

Thou knowest Lord the se_crets of our Hearts Shut not

Bass.

Grave. Thou knowest Lord the se_crets of our Hearts Shut not

Shut not thy merciful ears un_to our prayr's but spare us Lord spare us

Shut not thy merciful ears un_to our prayr's but spare us Lord spare us

Shut not thy merciful ears un_to our prayr's but spare us Lord spare us

Shut not thy merciful ears un_to our prayr's but spare us Lord spare us

Lord most Ho_ly O God O God most mighty O ho_ly and most

Lord most Ho_ly O God O God most mighty O ho_ly and most

Lord most Ho_ly O God O God most mighty O ho_ly and most

Lord most Ho_ly O God O God most mighty O ho_ly and most

merciful Saviour Thou most worthy Judge eternal suffer us not suf_

merciful Saviour Thou most worthy Judge e_ternal suffer us not suf_

merciful Saviour Thou most worthy Judge e_ternal suffer us not suf_

merciful Saviour Thou most worthy Judge e_ternal suffer us not suf_

_fer us not at our last hour for a__ny pains of death for a__ny

_fer us not at our last hour for a__ny pains of death for a__ny

_fer us not at our last hour for a__ny pains of

_fer us not at our last hour Organ for a__ny pains of

pains of death to fall to fall from thee. A___men.

pains of death to fall to fall from thee. A___men.

death of death to fall to fall from thee. A___men.

death ___ to fall to fall from thee. A___men.

DUETTO.

For two Sopranos.

Psalm. 47. Verse. 6ᵗʰ.   Pergolesi.

O sing Praises unto our God

O sing Praises un-to our King unto our God un-to our King sing

Praises to our God sing Praises to our King sing Praises to our God sing

6 6 7 6 6♮ 6   6 6 7 6   6   6 6 7 6 6♮ 6
    5 4   5   5   4

Praises to our King sing   Prai ― ― ― ― ― ― ― ― ― fes

6 6 7 6   Cres: for.
    5

to our King
6 5   6   4 6   6 6♮
4 ♮   5   2   4

S.   for.   pia.
S. for.   O sing Praises unto   our King sing
                                                         pia.
S. O sing Praises un-to   our God for.   sing
                          6 5♮   6 5   pia.

Praises to God sing Praises to our King   sing to our God

Praises to God sing Praises to our King   O sing   Prai ― ― ― ―
6 ♭7 ― ― ― 6♮ 5 6 8 7   6 for.   6   6 6 6   6
4   4 ♮ 4 6 5   5
         3

Organ
Organ
pia.
for.
fing unto our King
fing to our God
fing unto our King
fes
Cres:
fing ye Prai - - fes - - - O fing Prai - - fes to our God
fing ye Prai - - fes O fing Prai - - fes to our God
fing ye Prai - - fes O fing Prai - - fes to our King.
fing ye Prai - - fes O fing Prai - - fes to our King.

SOLO ANTHEM.

For a Soprano.

Psalm. 103.   Dr. Green.

Largo Andante.

Praife the Lord O__ my Soul Praife the Lord O__ my

Soul and all that is with_in me all all that is with_in me Praife

his Ho__ly Name Praife __ his Ho__ly Name

Who forgiveth all thy fin Who forgiveth all thy fin and

healeth all thine infir_mities heal_eth all _ _ _ heal_ _eth all _ _
_ _ _ thine_ _ _ in_fir_mi_ties
Chords pia.
pia.
Who faveth thy
fr.
pia.
life from de_ftruction Who fa_veth thy life thy life from de_ _
_ _ftruction and Crowneth thee with mer_ _cy and loving kind_ _nefs
Crowneth thee with mer_ _cy with mercy and loving kindnefs Crowneth thee with
mer_ _cy and loving kind_ _nefs
Organ
Praife the Lord O my
fr.
pia.

Organ
Soul Praise the Lord O my Soul
Organ
O my
for.
pia.
Soul Praise the Lord and forget not all - - forget not all his be - - ne - -
Organ
- - fits and forget not all his benefits forget not all his
for.
pia.
Organ
bene-fits all all forget not all his be - - ne - - fits.
for.
pia.
Organ pia.
Vivace
for.

O Praiſe the Lord ye An-gels of his ye
pia.
An-gels of his ye that ex-cel ex--cel--- in ſtrength
O Praiſe the Lord O Praiſe the Lord ye An-gels of his ye--
Organ
--- that ex-cel ex-cel in ſtrength that ful-
for.
pia.
--fil his Commandments his Commandments ye ſervants that
do his plea-ſure ye fer--vants that do his plea--

_ fure O Praife the Lord ye Angels of his ye that ex_
_ cel ex_cel in ftrength _ _ _ _
Organ ftr.
ftr.
that ful_fil his commandments his Commandments ye
pia.
Ser_vants that do his plea_ _ _ _
_ _ _ _ fure ye Ser_vants that do his plea_
ftr. Organ
_ fure
ftr.

DUETTO.
For two Tenors.

Psalm. 17. Verse. 2.   Marcello.

This Duetto may be sung by two Sopranos.

thy Command - ments Let me be Judg - ed
thy Command - ments with righteous
with righteous Judgment Come from thy
Judgment with righteous Judgment O let my Sentence
presence Come from thy pre-fence Come- from thy- - pre- -
O let my Sentence Come- - from thy- - pre- -
fence let me be Judg-ed with righteous Judgment
- - fence with righteous Judgment let me be Judg-ed
pia.
Cres:
for.

pia. *Cres:* *for.*

Come from thy pre_fence Come from thy prefence Come_

pia. *Cres:* *for.*

O let my Sentence O let my Sentence Come.

for.

_ _ _ from thy _ _ pre _ _ fence. Organ Fine.

_ _ from thy_ _ _ pre _ _ fence. Fine.

Lento.

O Shew thy lov_ing kind _ nefs

Lento.

Thy marvellous lov_ing

O Thou that art the Sa_ _ viour

kind _ _ nefs of them that trust in

Shew thy loving kind - - nefs of
Thee Thou that art the Sa - viour
them that trust in Thee Thou art the Sa - - viour of
that trust in Thee Thou art the Sa - - viour of
them that - - trust - - - in Thee Thou art the Sa - - viour
them that - - trust - - - in Thee Thou art the
of them that - - - trust - - - in Thee.
Sa - - viour of them that - - - trust - - - in Thee.
Da Capo
dal Segno
pia.
tr.

SOLO.
For a Tenor.

Psalm 144. Verse 2.   Handel.

Larghetto.

Ev'-ry day will I give

thanks   Ev'-ry day will I give thanks un-to Thee   un-to

Thee and praiſe thy name - - - - - - and praiſe thy name - -
- - - - - - and praiſe - - - - - - - - thy name for e-ver and
e - - - - ver - - - for ever and e - - - ver
for.
pia.
Ev'-ry day will I give thanks un--to Thee un-to Thee and

praise thy name for ever and e ver for
e-ver and e ver for e-ver and e
ver Ev'ry Day will I give thanks unto Thee and praise thy name for
e-ver and e ver for e-ver and e ver and

praise thy name   and praise

thy name for ever and e _ _ _ ver and praise thy name for

ever and e _ _ ver

ANTHEM.
For two Sopranos.

Psalm 34. Verse 1st.   King.

Moderato.   Organ.

I will al_way give thanks _ _ _ _ _ _ _ _ un_ _

I will al_way give thanks give thanks un_ _

_ _to the Lord I will alway give thanks un_ _to the Lord I will al_way give thanks

_ _ to the Lord I will alway give thanks un_ to the Lord

I will

I will al_way give thanks I will al_way give thanks un_ _

al_way give thanks I will al_way give thanks I will al_way give thanks un_ _

_ to the Lord His praise shall be e_ver in _ my mouth His praise shall be ever His

_ _ to the Lord His praise shall be e_ver in _ my mouth His praise shall be ever His

praise shall be e _ _ _ _ _ _ _ _ _ _ ver in _ my mouth His

praise shall be e _ _ _ _ _ _ _ _ ver in _ _ my mouth His

praise shall be ever His praise shall be e _ _ _ _ _ _ _ _ ver

praise shall be ever His praise shall be e _ _ _ _ _ _ _ ver

in _ my mouth.

in _ my mouth.

Solo. Second Soprano.

Recit: My Soul fhall make her boaft fhall make her boaft in the Lord my

Soul fhall make her boaft fhall make her boaft in the Lord the humble fhall hear there

- of the humble the humble fhall hear there of and be Glad the

humble the hum-ble fhall hear there of and be Glad

Solo. First Soprano.

Chearful. *Organ*

O praife the Lord praife the Lord with me *Organ*

O praife the Lord praife the Lord with . . me   O . . praife the

Lord   O . . praife . . . . the Lord with me   O praife the

Lord   O praife the Lord with me   O praife . . .

. . the Lord with me   O praife . . . . .

. the Lord with me O . . praife . . . . . the Lord with

me .   Volti

Duetto.

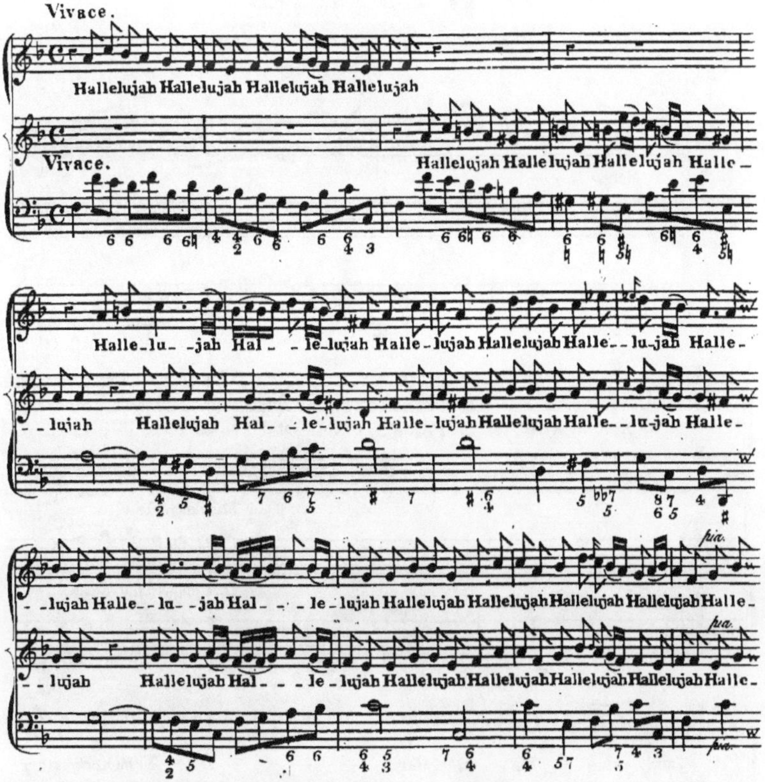

ANTHEM.

For an Alto, Tenor, and Bass.

Psalm 139.   Dr. Croft.

Alto.
an Octave
lower.

Slow   Organ

Tenor.
an Octave
lower.

Slow   7 6   4 3   6 6 6 6   4 6   4 3
                                        2

O Lord thou hast searched me   out   and known me

Thou knowest my down

Thou knowest my down

7 6   4 3   6 6 6 6

and mine __ up __ ri __ sing   Thou knowest my

sitting   O Lord thou hast searched me   out and known me

sitting   and mine up __ ri __ sing   Thou knowest my

6   6 5   ♯   7 6   6 5   4 ♯

This Anthem may be sung by two Sopranos and a Bass.

down - fitting and mine - - up - ri - - sing
and mine - - - up - ri - - sing and mine up -
down - - fitting O Lord Thou hast fearched me out and
Thou knoweft my down - - fitting O Lord Thou haft fearched me out - -
- rif - ing knoweft my down - - fitting and mine uprifing O Lord Thou haft fearched me
known me and mine uprifing O Lord Thou haft fearched me
- - Thou haft fearched me - - - out - - and known - - - me
out - - Thou haft fearched me out and known - - me
out - - haft fearched me out and known me Thou knowest my down
Tasto Solo

Thou knoweſt my down — ſitting and

and mine — — up — ri — ſing and mine up — ri — ſing

ſitt — ing and mine up — ri — ſing and mine up — — ri — — — ſing and

mine up — ri — ſing Thou under — ſtandest my thoughts

mine up — ri — ſing Thou under — ſtandest my

mine up — ri — ſing Thou under — ſtandest my

Thou under — ſtandest my thoughts long — — — before

thoughts under — ſtandest my thoughts long — — — before Thou under —

thoughts under — ſtandest my thoughts long — — — before

Thou under-ftan-deft my thoughts　Thou under-ftandeft my

-ftan-deft my thoughts　Thou under-ftan-deft my thoughts long-

Thou under-ftandeft my thoughts　Thou under-

thoughts long before　Thou under-ftandeft my thoughts long - - - be-

-before Thou under-ftandeft my thoughts long - - - be-

-ftandeft my thoughts long - - - be-fore　long - - - - be-

Organ

-fore.

-fore.

-fore.

Solo Bass.

Chords pia.
Organ
Moderato.
for.
pia.
Thou art about my
path and a.. bout.. my bed Thou art about my path and a..
..bout.. my bed
Chords pia.
for.
Thou art about my path and a.. bout.. my Bed Thou
art about my path and a.. bout my Bed and spi.. est out

Chorus pia.
pia.
all my ways For lo For
for.
for.
lo there is not a word in my tongue but Thou O Lord knowest it
pia.
all - - - - - to - - ge - ther there is not a word in my
Chorus pia.
tongue but Thou O Lord knowest it all - - - - - to - - gether
for.
Thou art about my
pia.
path and a - - bout my Bed Thou art about my path and a - -

-bout my Bed and fpi..eft out all - my ways for

lo for. for lo! there is not a

word in my tongue but Thou O Lord knoweft it all - - to-gether for

lo there is not a word in my tongue but Thou O

Lord knoweft it all - - - - - - to-gether Thou O

Lord knoweft it all - - - - - - to-ge--ther

Solo Alto.

Slow.

pia.

Whither shall I — go then from thy Spirit or whither shall I

go — whi—ther shall I go — — then from — thy

presence

whither ſhall I - - go then from thy Spirit or whither ſhall I go - - then whither ſhall I
go - then whither ſhall I go then from - - thy preſence or whither ſhall I
pia.
go - - then whither ſhall I go - - then whither ſhall I go then from - - - thy
preſence If I climb up into Heav'n Thou art there If I go down to Hell Thou art
there - - al - ſo O whither ſhall I go - - then whither ſhall I go then from thy
preſence If I climb up into Heav'n Thou art there If I climb up into Heav'n Thou art

there   If I go down to Hell Thou art there — — &c   O whither shall I

go   whither shall I go   whither shall I go from thy Spirit   or

whither shall I go   whither shall I go   whither shall I go then from . .

— — thy Presence   whither shall I go   whither shall I go   whither shall I

go then from . . thy presence   If I take the Wings of the morning   If I take the

Wings of the morning and remain in the uttermost parts of the Sea

Organ
Moderato.
Thy right hand ſhall
Even there _ _ al_ _ ſo ſhall Thy hand _ _
Moderato.
lead me
lead me and Thy right hand ſhall hold me
and Thy
and Thy right hand ſhall hold me Even there _ _ _ al_ _ ſo ſhall Thy
Even there _ _ al_ _ ſo ſhall Thy hand _ _ _
right hand ſhall hold me
hand _ _ lead me
and Thy right hand ſhall

hold me andThy right hand ſhall hold me Thy right hand ſhall hold me
andThy right hand ſhall hold me Even there - - -
hold me andThy right hand ſhall hold me Thy right hand ſhall hold me
6 5 7 ♯ 6
andThy righthand ſhall hold me
al - ſo ſhallThy hand - - lead me andThy right hand ſhall hold me andThy
Even there - - - al - ſo ſhallThy - hand - - - lead me andThy
4 3 6 6 4 5 3 9 4 8 3
Thy right hand Thy right hand ſhall hold me
righthand ſhall hold me Thy right hand Thy right hand ſhall hold me
righthand ſhall hold me Thy right hand Thy right hand ſhall hold me
6 6 6 6 7 5 4 7

ANTHEM.

For two Sopranos.

Psalm 103.   **Solo. first Soprano.**   William Savage.

Lively.

Praise the Lord. O my Soul and all that is with_in me Praise his ho_ly name Praise the Lord O my Soul and all and

all that is with_in me Praife
his ho_ly name
Organ
Praife the
for.
pia.
Lord O my Soul and all that is with_in me Praife his
Organ
ho_ly name
fr.
for.
Slow
Who fa_veth thy life thy life from de_ftruction who
fa_veth thy life thy life from de_ftruction

46

DUETTO.

Very Slow.

For He know-eth where-of we are made He re-mem-breth that we — are — but dust He re-mem-breth He re-mem-breth that we — are — but dust.

Organ

Chearful.
Second Soprano
O - - - ſpeak ſpeak good of the Lord - - - all - - ye works of
O - - ſpeak ſpeak good of the Lord - - - all - - ye works - - of
His
His In all places of His Domi - - nion in all places of
In all places of His Domi - - nion in all places of

his Domi- - -nion O- - - Speak good of the
his Domi- -nion O- - - Speak good of the Lord O- - -
Lord O Speak good of the Lord all ye works of His In all
- - - Speak good of the Lord all ye works ye works of His In all
places of His Domi- -nion in all places of his Domi- - -nion.
Organ
places of His Domi- -nion in all places of his Domi- - -nion.

SOLO.

For an Alto.

Psalm. 8.　　　　　　　　　　Marcello.

Allegro moderato.

O Lord our Governor O - - how excellent is thy great name O how excellent is thy great name in all the world O how excellent in all - - the

Chorus.
Organ
for.
world O how excellent in all the world
pia.
Solo.
O Lord our
Governor O - - - how excellent O - - - how excellent
In all the world is thy great name O - - how
Chorus.
ex - cel - lent is thy great name O Lord our Governor
O - - how excellent O - - how excellent in all the

world is thy great name O - - how ex - cel - lent
Solo.
is thy great name O - - - - Lord - - - - - our - - - - -
Go - - - - ver - - - - - nor - - - O - - how ex - cel - lent
Chorus.
is thy great name O - - how ex - cel - lent is thy great
fòr.
Organ
name.
fòr.
pia.

Solo.
Thou O Je - ho - vah haſt set _ _ thy Glo - ry a - bove _ _ the Heavens haſt ſet _ _ thy

Glo - ry a _ _ bove the Heav'ns!

Chorus.
Thou O Je - ho _ vah haſt ſet _ _ thy Glo - ry a - bove _ the Heavens haſt ſet _ thy

Chorus.
Glo - ry haſt ſet _ _ thy Glo - ry a _ _ bove _ _ the Heav'ns haſt

fet _ _ _ thy Glo - ry a _ _ bove _ _ the Heav'ns DaCapo dal Segno.

54

DUETTO.
For two Sopranos.

Psalm 23rd.   Dr. Greene.

feed me in green pastures He shall feed me in green pastures And lead me

pastures in green pastures And lead me forth lead me

9 8 6 5 6 4 6 6 9 8 6 7 6 7
4 3 4 3 #

forth beside the waters the waters of Comfort of Comfort He shall lead me lead me

forth beside the waters the waters of Comfort He shall lead me

6 5 6 6 6 5 7 6 9 7 5 6
4 3 # # # 5

forth beside the waters of com __ fort He __ shall lead me

He shall lead me shall lead __ me lead me forth be-side the

6 6 6 5 6 7 6 6 7
4 4 4 5 #

Organ.

He __ shall lead me lead me forth beside the wa __ ters of com __ fort

wa __ ters of com __ fort beside the wa __ ters of com __ fort

7 6 7 4 6 7 6 6
4 # 4
2

He shall convert my soul _ _ convert my

He shall convert my soul my

soul and bring me in the paths the paths of righteous_nefs

soul and bring me in the paths the paths of righteous_nefs

He shall convert my soul & bring me bring me in the paths the

He shall convert my soul _ _ my soul _ _ and bring me in the paths the

paths of righteousnefs for _ His name_fake for _ His name_

paths of righteousnefs for His name_fake for _ His name_

- - fake. The Lord is my Shepherd there -
- - fake. there - - fore can I want nothing
- - fore can I want nothing there - - fore can I - - - no - - thing
there - - fore can I no - - thing no - - thing
want. The Lord is my She - - pherd there - - fore can I - -
want. The Lord is my Shepherd there - fore can I no - - thing
no - - thing want. there - - fore can I no - - thing want.
no - - thing want. there - - fore can I no - - thing want.

SOLO.

For a Soprano.

Psalm 42. Verse 3.   Handel.

Un poco Adagio.

pia.   for.   pia.   for.

pia.   for.   pia.   for.

pia.

Tears

pia.

Tears are my dai_ _ly dai_ _ly food

Tears _ _ _ _ are my dai_ _ly dai_ _ly

food my dai_ _ly food my dai_ _ly

food while thus they fay while thus while thus they

say Where is now thy God   Where is now thy God   Where is now thy

God   Where   Where   Where is now thy God

Tears

Tears are my dai — — — — — ly food   Tears are

my dai--ly food ___ while thus they fay ___ while thus they

for.   pia.   for.   pia.   for.

fay   where is now thy God   Where is now thy God

for.   for.   pia.   for.

pia.

where   where   where   where _____

for.   pia.   Adagio

now thy God   where   where is now thy God

pia.   Adagio

DUETTO.
for two Sopranos.

Psalm 34. Verse 11.   Steffani.

Moderato. Organ.

Come ye Children and hearken to me........ Come ye Children and hearken to me I will teach you the fear of the Lord I will teach you the me I will teach you the fear of the Lord the

fear of the Lord.
fear of the Lord. Come ye Children and hearken to
Come ye Children and hearken to me I will
me I will teach you the
pia.
teach you the fear of the Lord the fear of the Lord. Come ye
fear of the Lord of the Lord the fear of the Lord.
pia.
Children Come ye Children and hearken to me hearken to

for.
me Come ye Children will teach you the
for.
Come ye Children hearken to me I will teach you the
fear of the Lord
pia.
fear of the Lord I will teach you the fear of the
pia.
pia.
I will teach you the fear of the Lord of - - - - the
Cres:
Cres:
Lord I - - - - - - will teach you - - - - - - - the fear of the
Cres:
tr
pia.
Lord Come ye Children and hearken un - - to me
pia.
for.
Lord Come ye Children I will
pia.
for.

for.
pia.
I will teach you the fear of the Lord I will
teach you the fear the fear of the Lord
pia.
Cres:
teach you the fear of the Lord I - - - - - - - - will teach you - -
pia.
Cres.
I will teach you the fear of the
Cres:
for
Organ pia.
- - - - the fear of the Lord
for.
Lord the fear of the Lord
for.
pia.

ANTHEM.
For a Soprano and Bass.

Psalm 3 Verse 4th. Solo Soprano. Marcello.

Organ.

Adagio.

7 6   7 6   5 b7 6   7 6   6 5 8 7

pia.

In my distrefs I cal_led up_on the Lord Je__ho_vah

pia.   7 6   6   7 6

Cres.

In my distrefs I called upon Je__ho_vah and he did bear me out_

6 5   6   4 3   6 4   Cres. 6
4 3   5 7

pia.   Cres.   for.

__ of his ho_ly Hill I call'd in my distrefs upon Jeho_vah and he did

pia.

7 6 5   4 3 4 2   6   6 4   for. 6

This Anthem may be Sung by two Sopranos.

bear me out of _ His ho _ ly Hill

SOLO BASS,

Psalm. 8ᵗʰ Verse. 4ᵗʰ

Lento

What is a Mortal O _ _ Je _ hovah that Thou art

mindful art mindful of Him and the Son _ _ of a Mortal

that Thou vi_sitest him Thou vi_si_test him

That Thou art mindful art mindful of him and the

Son of a Mor_tal that Thou vi_si_test him Thou visi_test

him.

DUETTO.

Psalm 7. Verse 18. Recit.

Soprano.
I will give thanks unto the Lord according to his righteous_nefs.

Bass.
according to his righteous_nefs.

Allegro.
I will sing_ _ _

I will sing_ _ I will sing prai _ _ _ _ _ _ _ _ _ses

Allegro.

I will sing prai _ _ _ _ _ _ _ _ _ _ ses

will sing praises sing prai _ _ _ _ ses un_to the

for.
unto the name of the Lord most high the Lord most high.

name of the Lord_ _ most_ _ High_ _ _ the Lord most high.

pia.
for.
will fing praifes fing prai - - - - - - fes I will
pia.
I will fing - - - I will fing prai - - - - - - - - -
pia.
fing - - I will fing prai - - - - - - - - - - fes I will
- - - fes will fing praifes fing prai - - - - - fes
fing - - I will fing prai - - - - - - - - - - - - fes
will fing prai - fes I will fing prai - fes I will fing prai - -
un - to the name of the Lord - - most - - high - - -
- - - - - - - - fes un - to the name of the Lord most

ffor.
un_to the Lord most high I will fing _ _ I will fing
ffor.
high the Lord most high will fing praifes fing,
ffor.
prai _ _ _ _ _ _ _ _ _ _ _ _ fes will fing praifes fing prai _ _ _
pia.
Cres.
praifes I will fing _ _ I will fing prai _ _ _ _ _ _ _ _
for.
_ _ _ _ _ _ _ _ _ _ fes un_to the name of the Lord _ _ _ _ _
_ _ _ _ _ _ _ _ _ _ fes I will fing _ _ _
_ _ _ most high will fing praifes fing prai _ _ _ _ _ _ fes I will
I will fing prai _ _ _ _ _ _ fes will fing praifes fing prai _ _ _

sing   will sing praises sing

fes un__to the name of the Lord

prai   fes un__to the

most High

name of the Lord

will sing praises sing prai

most high

fes un__to the name of the

un--to the name of the Lord most High to the name of the

Lord _ _ _ _ _ _ _ _ _ _ _ the _

Lord the name of the Lord most High to the name of the

_Lord _ _ _ _ _ _ _ _ most

Lord the Lord_ _ _ most High.

High to the Lord _ _ most _ _ High.

ANTHEM.

For four Voices.

Psalm 22d. Reynolds.

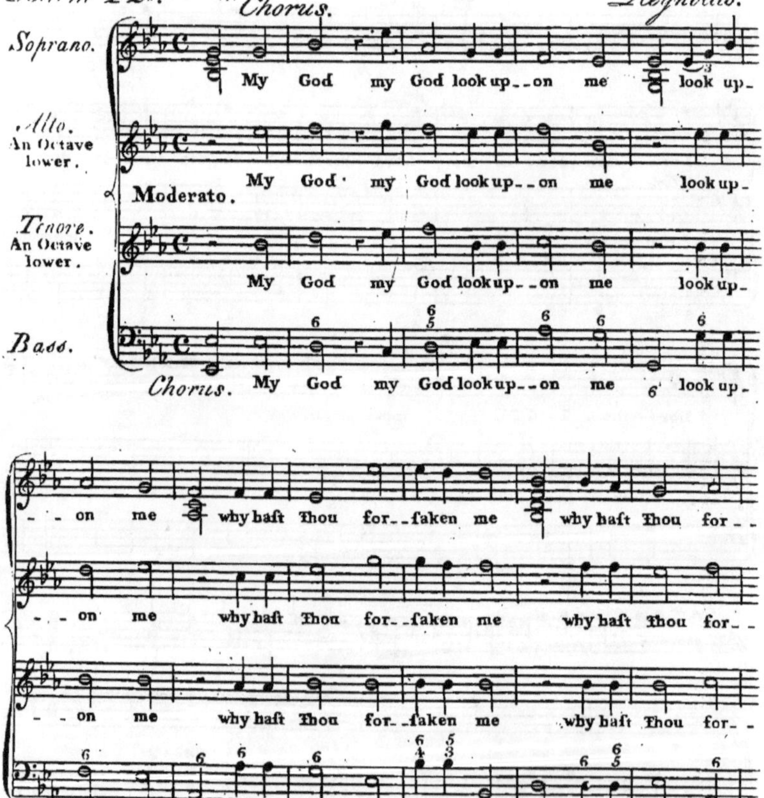

faken me and art fo far from my health and from the words of

faken me and art fo far from my health and from the words of my com-

faken me and art fo far from my health and from the

faken me and art fo far from my health and from the words of my com-

my complaint the words of my complaint and from the

-plaint the words of my complaint and from the words of

words of my complaint the words of my com-plaint

-plaint and from the words of my com-plaint and from the

words of my complaint the words of my com-plaint

my com-plaint the words of my com-plaint

and from the words of my complaint the words of my com-plaint

words of my com-plaint and from the words of my com-plaint

DUETTO.

Largo Andante.

Soprano 1. O — my God I cry in the day time but

Soprano 2.

Largo Andante. 6   6   4   6   6   6   7   6
                    4   2   5

Thou hearest not.

O — my God I cry in the day time but

6   6   6   6   6   7   6   6
4   2

                       but Thou hear—est not but

Thou hear—est not but Thou hear—est not but

6   6   6   6   6
4   4

Thou hear—est not   and in the Night

Thou hear—est not and in the Night sea—son al—

6   6   6   6   6
                                      5

fea-fon al-fo I take no rest no
-fo I take no reft I take no
9 8 9 6 5 6 4 4 2 6 6
reft I take no reft al-fo I take I
reft no reft al-fo I take I
6 4 4 2 6 6 5 7 3 6 4 7 5 6 4 7 5 7
piu
take no reft I take no reft no
piu
take no reft no reft I take no
6 4 3 piu 6 6 4 4 2 6 6 5
reft al-fo I take I take no reft.
reft al-fo I take I take no reft.
7 6 4 7 5 6 4 7 7 6 4 5 3

Andante. Chorus.

But Thou conti..nu..est Ho..ly   O thou Worship of Is..ra..

But Thou conti..nu..est Ho..ly   O thou Worship of Is..ra..

But Thou conti..nu..est Ho..ly   O thou Worship of Is..ra..

Andante But Thou conti..nu..est Ho..ly   O thou Worship of Is..ra..

..el.   Thou con..ti..nu..est Ho..ly   O..thou Worship of

..el.   Thou con..ti..nu..est Ho..ly   O..thou Worship of

..el.   Thou con..ti..nu..est Ho..ly   O..thou Worship of

..el.   Thou con..ti..nu..est Ho..ly   O..thou Worship of

Is..ra..el.   O..thou Worship of Is..ra..el.

Is..ra..el.   O..thou Worship of Is..ra..el.

Is..ra..el.   O..thou Worship of Is..ra..el.

Is..ra..el.   O..thou Worship of Is..ra..el.

ANTHEM.
For four Voices.

Farrant

Slow. *Chorus.*

Soprano.
Lord for thy ten-der mer-cies fake lay

Alto.
An Octave
lower.
Lord for thy ten-der mer--cies fake lay

Tenor.
An Octave
lower.
Lord for thy ten-der mer--cies fake lay

Bass.
Chorus.
Slow. Lord for thy ten-der mer--cies fake lay

not our Sins to our Charge But for--give that is paft and give us

not our Sins to our Charge But for--give that is paft and give us

not our Sins to our Charge But for--give that is paft and give us

not our Sins to our Charge But for--give that is paft and give us

Grace to amend our Sin—ful lives. To de—cline from Sin And in—

Grace to a—mend our Sin—ful lives. To de—cline from Sin And in—

Grace to a—mend our Sin—ful lives. To de—cline from Sin And in—

Grace to a—mend our Sin—ful lives. To de—cline from Sin And in—

—cline to Vir—tue—— That we may walk with a

—cline to Vir—tue That we may walk with a per—fect

—cline to Vir—tue That we may walk with a per—fect heart a per—fect

—cline to Vir—tue That we may walk with a per—fect heart with a per—fect

per—fect Heart—— That we may walk with a per—fect Heart be—

Heart That we may walk with a per—fect Heart be—

heart That we may walk with a per—fect Heart with a per—fect Heart be—

Heart That we may walk with a per—fect Heart with a per—fect Heart be—

for.
- - fore Thee now and e- - ver - - more. That
for.
- fore Thee now and e- - ver - - - more. That we may
for.
- - fore Thee now and e- - ver- - more. That we may walk with a per - fect
for.
- - fore Thee now and e- - ver- - more. That we may walk with a per - fect
we may walk with a per - fect Heart - - - That we may walk with a
walk with a per - fect Heart That we may walk with a
heart a per - fect Heart That we may walk with a per - fect Heart with a
heart with a per - fect Heart That we may walk with a per - fect Heart with a
per - - fect Heart be - fore Thee now and e- - ver - - more.
per - - fect Heart be - fore Thee now and e- - ver - - more.
per - - fect Heart be - - fore Thee now and e- - ver - - more.
per - - fect Heart be - fore Thee now and e- - - ver - - more.

SOLO.
For a Bass.

Psalm 68 Verse 2.   Handel.

Like as the smoke va _ _ _ _ _ _ nishes

So shal Thou drive _ _

them a _ way
fo fhalt Thou drive them a _
way
a _ way
a _ way fo fhalt Thou drive
them a _
tr
fr.
way
pia.
Like as the fmoke
fr.
pia.
Like as the fmoke

As the smoke va nisheth so shalt Thou drive

them so shalt Thou drive them a - way. so shalt Thou

T.S.

drive them a - way a - way. a - way so shalt Thou drive them a - way

pp.

so shalt Thou drive them

so shalt thou drive them a _ way. so shalt thou drive them a _ _ way _ _ _

so shalt thou drive them a _ _ way.

ANTHEM.
For an Alto and Tenor.

Psalm 86. Verse 6.

Dr Green.

Alto. an Octave lower.

Tenor. an Octave lower.

Largo.

O — Lord give ear un — to my pray'r

Lord give ear un — to my pray'r O —

O — Lord give ear give ear un — to my pray'r.

Lord give ear give ear — un — to my pray'r. And

And ponder the

ponder the Voice of my humble desires the Voice — of my humble desires

This Anthem may be sung by two Sopranos, the lowest Voice taking the upper Stave an Octave lower, the higher Voice the Second Stave.

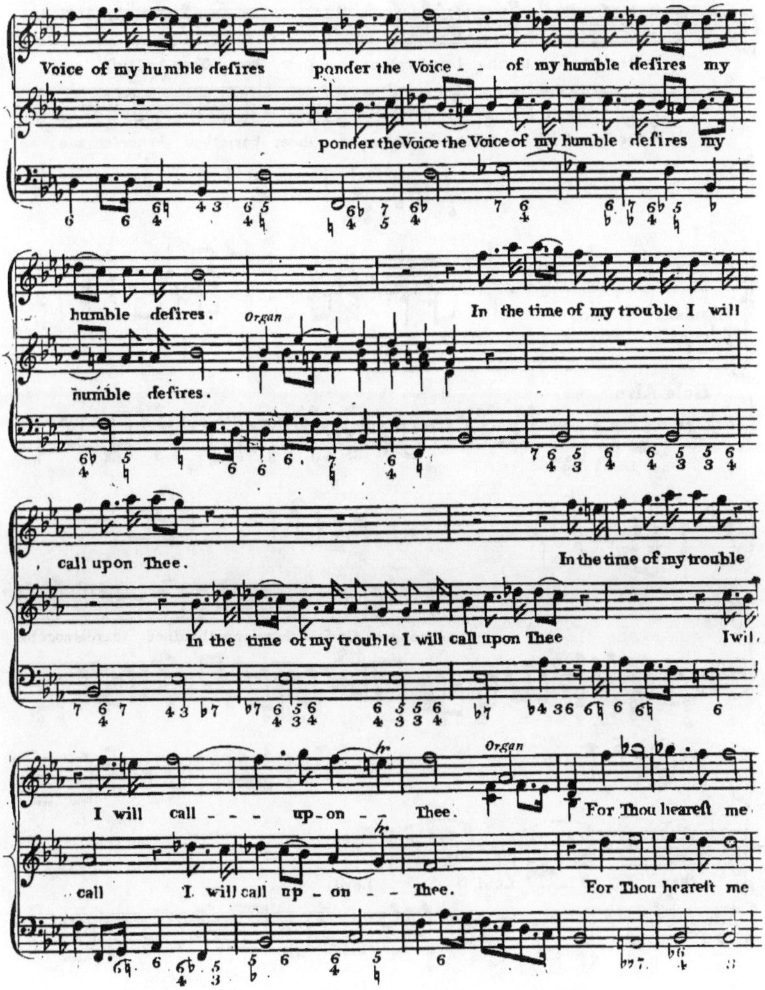

In the time of my trouble I will call upon Thee. For Thou hearest me.

In the time of my trouble I will call upon Thee. For Thou hearest me.

Andante Vivace.

Solo Alto.

Among the Gods there is none like Thee there is none like

thee O — Lord O — — Lord.

Among the Gods there is none like Thee there is none like Thee O — Lord O — Lord there is not One that can do as Thou doest there is not One that can do as Thou doest O —

- - - - Lord O - - - - - Lord there is not One that can do as Thou
doest O - - - - - Lord O - - - - - Lord there is - - not
One that can do as Thou doest.

DUETTO.

Vivace.

Organo

All

All Nations whom Thou hast

Nations whom Thou hast made shall come and worship Thee O Lord

made shall come and worship Thee O Lord _ _ _ _ O _ _ _

All Na-tions whom Thou hast made shall come and

Lord _ _ _ _ _ Lord

Organo

All

worship Thee O Lord

Na_tions whom Thou haſt made ſhall come and wor _ ſhip Thee O Lord
All Nations all Nations whom Thou haſt made ſhall come and
and ſhall Glo _ _ _ ri _ _ fy Thy Name ſhall
worſhip Thee O Lord and ſhall Glo _ _ _ ri _ _ fy Thy Name
Glo _ _ _ _ _ _ _ _ _ _ _ _ _ ri _ _ fy Thy Name _ _
ſhall Glo _ _ _ _ _ _ _ _ ri _ fy ſhall glori _ _ fy Thy Name _ _
Organ
ſhall Glo _ _ ri _ _ fy Thy Name All
All na _ _ tions whom Thou haſt

Na__tions whom Thou hast made All Na__tions shall come and
made All Na__tions whom Thou hast made shall come and
worship Thee O Lord And shall Glo__ri_fy Thy
worship Thee O Lord And shall Glo__ri_fy Thy
Name, shall Glo
Name, shall Glo
Adagio
ri__fy__Thy Name. shall Glo_ri__fy__Thy Name.
Adagio
ri__fy__Thy Name. shall Glo_ri__fy__Thy Name.
Adagio

DUETTO.

For an Alto, and Tenor.

Psalm 13 Vers. 6.   *Marcello.*

Allegro moderato.

And with Songs I will Ce _ lebrate the Name of Je

Tenor an Octave lower

_ ho _ _ _ _ _ vah _ _ _ _ _ _ will Ce_lebrate the

And with Songs I will Ce _ _ lebrate the Name of Je _ ho _ _ _

Name will Ce _ le_brate the   Name   will Ce _ le_brate the

_ _ _ vah   will Ce _ _ le_brate the Name will Ce _ le_brate the

THE DUETTO may be Sung by two Sopranos, the lowest Voice taking the upper Stave.

pia.
for.
Name of Je--ho--vah--most High the Name of Je--ho----vah
pia.
for.
Name of Je--ho--vah--most High the Name of Je-
pia.
And with Songs I will Ce---le--brate will Ce-lebrate the
--ho--vah will Ce-lebrate the Name will Ce-lebrate the Name
Name will Ce-lebrate the Name will Ce-lebrate the
the Name of Je--ho------vah will Ce-lebrate the
Name will Ce--lebrate the Name the Name of Je--
Name will Ce--le-brate the Name will Ce--lebrate the Name and with

ho — — — — — vah   And with Songs I will Ce — — lebrate

Songs I will — Ce — Celebrate the Name of Je — ho — — — — — vah — —

— the Name of Je — — ho — — — — — vah — — — — —

will Ce — — lebrate the   Name will Ce — — le — brate the

will Ce — lebrate the Name will Ce — lebrate the   Name of Je — ho — — vah —

name   will Ce — — lebrate the Name of Je — — ho — — vah — —

— — — moft   High   will Ce — lebrate the Name

— — — moft High will Ce — lebrate the Name   will Ce — lebrate the will Ce_lebrate the Name ... And with Songs I will

Name ... will Ce_lebrate the Name the Name of Je_ho__vah

6
4 ... 6 ... 6 6 6
4 4

Ce _ le__brate will Ce_lebrate the Name will Ce_lebrate the Name

the Name of Je_ho _ _ _ _ _ _ vah _ _ _ will Ce_lebrate the

6 ... 5 ... 6 ... 6
4 ... 3 ... 4

pia. ... _for._

will Ce_lebrate the Name of Je__ho__vah _ _ moſt High the Name of Je_

for.

Name will Ce_lebrate the Name ... And with Songs I will

pia. ... _for._

7 ... 6 6 ... 6 7 4 3
4 ... 5

pia.

_ho _ _ _ _ _ _ _ _ _ vah _ _ _ will Ce_lebrate the

Ce__lebrate will Ce_lebrate the Name will Ce_lebrate the Name

6 ... 6 ... 6
4 ... 4 ... 3 ... 4 ... 3

name and with Songs I will Ce_ _lebrate will Ce_lebrate the
pia.
will Ce_lebrate the Name the Name of Je_ _ho _ _ _ _ _ _vah _ _ _ _
pia.
Name will Ce_lebrate the Name will Ce_lebrate the Name
for.
_ _the Name of Je_ _ho _ _ _ _ _ _ _ _vah _ _ _ _ will Ce_lebrate the
for.
will Ce_lebrate the Name of Je_ _ho_ _ _vah_ _ most High
pia.
Name will Ce_lebrate the Name of Je_ _ho_ _ _vah_ _ most High will Ce_lebrate the
pia.
for.
will Ce_lebrate the Name of Je_ho_vah will Ce_lebrate the
for.
Name of Je_ _ho_vah of Je_ _ho_ _vah
pia.

Name will Ce_lebrate the Name of Je__ho__vah__ moſt High of__ Je_

will Ce_lebrate the Name of Je__ho__vah__ moſt High of Je_

5 7   6 7 8   6 6 6 6 7 6 7
3   5   5 6   4 4

_ho_vah__ moſt High of__ Je_ho__vah__ moſt High.

__ho_vah__moſt High___ of Je_ho__vah__ moſt High.

7 7 6 7   6 6 6 7 6 7 7 — 6 7
          4 4

tr. Organ for.

TRIO.

For an Alto, Tenor, and Bass.

Psalm 56 Verse 10.   Purcell.

In — God's word will I Re — joice —

In — God's word will I Re — joice —

In — God's word will I Re — joice —

in the Lord's word will I Com — fort me —

in the Lord's word will I Com — fort me —

in the Lord's word will I Com — fort me —

This TRIO may be Sung by two Sopranos and a Bass.

In God's Word will I Re - joice

In God's Word will I Re - joice

In God's Word will I Re - joice

In the Lord's Word will I Com - fort - me

In the Lord's Word will I Com - fort - me

In the Lord's Word will I Com - fort - me

Yea in God have I put - my truft I will not be - a -

Yea in God have I put - my truft I will not be - a -

Yea in God have I put - my truft I will not be - a -

_fraid what Man can do un __ to me I willnot be _ a __

_fraid what Man can do un __ to me I willnot be _ a __

_ fraid what Man can do un _ to me I willnot be _ a __

_ fraid what Man can do un _ to me I willnot be _ a __

_fraid what Man can do un _ _ to me. Yea in

_fraid what Man can do un _ _ to me. Yea in

_fraid what Man can do un _ _ to me. Yea in

_fraid what Man can do un _ _ to me. Yea in

God have I put _ _ _ _ my _ _ truft I willnot be _ _ a _

God have I put _ _ _ my _ _ truft I will not be _ a _

God have I put _ _ _ my _ _ truft I will not be _ a _

God have I put _ _ _ my _ _ truft I will not be _ a _

MISS WHITEHEAD'S

Sacred Music

Dedicated to his Grace

The ARCHBISHOP of CANTERBURY

Consisting of

Selections from the great English & Italian

MASTERS

Handel, Purcel, Green, Croft

MARCELLO, STEFFANI, PERGOLESE &c

the whole

Selected, Adapted & Arranged, for

One Two Three or Four Voices

and the

Piano Forte or Organ

By

R. J. S. STEVENS.

Organist of the Charterhouse & Temple, Gresham Professor &c.

in 3 Vol?

Vol.1.
Pr. 1. 1. 0.

London, Printed & Sold by PRESTON, at his Wholesale Warehouses 97, Strand.

INDEX to VOLUME II.

DUETTO.

For two Sopranos.

Psalm 9th.   Steffani.

I will give thanks un—to Thee O— Lord will give

I will give

thanks—— O——Lord will give thanks with—my whole

thanks un—to Thee O——Lord will give thanks with—my whole

Heart   I will give

Heart   I   will give thanks un—to Thee O——Lord will give

This Duetto may be Sung by two Tenors.

thanks un - to Thee   O _ Lord will give   thanks with _ my whole

thanks _ _ _   O _ _ _ Lord will give   thanks with _ _ my whole

Heart   I will give thanks un - to Thee   O _ _ Lord

Heart   I will give

I will give thanks un - to Thee   O _ _

thanks un - to Thee   O _ Lord will give   thanks _ _ _ O _ _ _

Lord will give   thanks with _ my whole _ heart   I will

Lord will give   thanks with _ _ my whole heart I will   Speak will

Organ.
Speak of all - thy mar - vel - lous Works
Speak of all - thy mar - vel - lous Works
pia.
I will give
pia.
pia.
I will give thanks un - to Thee O - -
thanks un - to Thee O - - Lord
Cres:
fr.
Lord will give thanks - - - - O - - Lord will give thanks with
Cres:
fr.
I will give thanks un - to Thee O - - Lord will give thanks with
Cres:
fr.

... my whole heart will give thanks will give thanks with

... my whole heart will give thanks will give thanks with

... my whole Heart. I will be

... my whole Heart.

glad and re — joice — re — joice — in Thee yea my Songs will I

make of Thy Name .... O Thou most High.

I will be

glad and re — — joice — re — — joice — in Thee yea my Songs will I —

make of thy Name — — — — — — — — — O Thou moſt

for. I will be glad and re — — joice — — re — joice — — in Thee yea my

for. High I will be glad and re — — joice — — in Thee — — O

So — gs will — I make of Thy Name — — — — — — — — — — O —

— — — Thou moſt High — — — — will re — joice — — — O — —

pia.
Thou - most high yea - my Songs will I - make of - Thy -
Thou - most high yea - my Songs will I - make of - Thy -
Name of Thy - Name - - O - - Thou most high yea - - my
Name of Thy - Name - - O - - Thou most high yea - - my
for.
Songs will I - make of Thy - Name of Thy - Name O -
Songs will I - make of Thy - Name of Thy - Name O -
Adagio
- - - Thou most high O - - Thou - most high
- - Thou most high O - - Thou - most high

DUETTO.

For two Sopranos.

Psalm 46th Verse 5th   Dr. Green.

For God is in the midst of us therefore shall we not be mo_

For God is in the midst of us therefore shall we not be mo_ved   For God   is

_ved   For God   is

in   the midst   of us therefore shall we   not be moved   therefore   shall

in   the midst   of us therefore shall we   not be moved   therefore   shall

This Duetto may be sung by two Tenors.

we not - be mo_ved For God is in the midſt of us For God is in the midſt of
we not_ be mo_ved is in the midſt of us is in the midſt of
us therefore ſhall we not be mo_ved therefore ſhall we not be
us therefore ſhall we not be mo_ved therefore ſhall we not be
mo_ved God is our hope and re_fuge God is our hope and
mo_ved God is our hope and re_fuge God is our hope and
refuge our hope and re_ fuge therefore ſhall we _ ſhall we not be
refuge our hope and re_ fuge there_fore ſhall we _ ſhall we _ not be

moved ſhall not be mo - - - - - - ved we ſhall not be mo - -
moved ſhall not be mo - - - - - ved we ſhall not be mo - -
- - ved God is - - our hope - God is our hope and re - -
- - ved our hope God is our hope and re -
- - fuge God is - - our hope - God is our hope and re - fuge
- fuge our hope our hope our hope and re - - fuge
Organ
pia.
for.

SOLO.
For a Soprano.

Psalm 68th Verse 3d. Handel.

Let the righteous be glad and rejoice and rejoice before God Let the righteous be glad and rejoice

This Solo may be sung by a Tenor.

And re_joice
And rejoice
and rejoice before the
Lord
Let the
for.
pia.
righteous be glad and re_joice

And re _ _joice _ _ _ _ _ _ _ _ _ _ _

And rejoice be_fore God

Let the righteous be glad _ _ Let the

righteous re_ _joice _ _ _ _

and rejoice _ _ _ _ _ _ _ _ _ _ _ _

_ _ _ _ and rejoice be _ fore God

Let them alfo be merry and joyful let them alfo be mer _ ry and

joyful merry and joyful let them al _ fo be mer _ ry and

joyful and joy
for.
ful
Let them
pia.
alſo be merry and joyful merry and joy
ful merry and
pia.
for.
Joy

ful   merry   and joyful let them alfo be merry and

joyful be merry and   joy _ _ _ _ ful   for.

SANCTUS & KYRIE ELEESON.

For Four Voices.

From the Communion Service.   Dr. Orlando Gibbons.

Slow.

Lord — have mercy up—on — us — and in—cline our
hearts to keep this — law. Lord have mercy up—on — us and write
all these Thy laws in our hearts we be — seech — Thee

Lord — have mercy up—on — us and in—cline our
hearts to keep this — law. Lord have mercy up—on — us and
write all these Thy laws in — our hearts we beseech — Thee

Lord — have mercy up—on — us and in—cline our hearts to
keep — this — law. Lord have mer—cy upon us and write
all these Thy — laws — in our hearts we be—seech — Thee

Lord — have mercy up—on — us and in—cline our
hearts to keep this — law. Lord have mercy up—on — us and write
all these Thy laws in our hearts we be—seech — Thee

NUNC DIMITTIS.

For Four Voices.

Luke 2. Verse 29.

Dr. Orlando Gibbons.

thy fal - va - tion which Thou haft - - pre - pa - - red be - fore - -
- - fal - va - - tion which Thou - - haft prepa - - red be - fore - the
Thy fal - - va - tion which Thou haft pre - - pa - - red be - - - fore -
- - fal - va - - tion which Thou haft pre - pa - - - - red be -
Organ:
- - the face of - - all people To be a light to ligh - ten the Gentiles
face - - of all - people To be a light to lighten the Gentiles
- - the face of all - people To be a light to lighten the Gentiles
- - fore the face of all - people To be a light to lighten the Gentiles
and to be the Glo - ry of Thy people - If - - ra - - - el.
and to be the Glo - - ry of Thy people If - - ra - - - el.
and to be the Glo - ry of Thy people If - - ra - - el.
and to be the Glo - - ry of - Thy people If - - - ra - - - el

Canon Two in One,
Organ.

Glo __ ry be to the Fa __ ther and to __ the Son

Glo __ ry be to the Fa __ ther and

Glo __ ry be __ __ to the Fa __ ther and to __ __ the __ __

Glo __ ry be to the Fa __ ther and to the

And to the Ho __ ly Ghost As it was in the be __ gin __

to the Son And to the Ho __ ly Ghost __ As it was in

Son And to the Ho __ __ __ ly Ghost As it was in the be __

Son And to the Ho __ __ __ ly Ghost As it was in the be __

__ ning is __ __ now and ever fhall be world

the be __ __ gin __ __ ning is __ __ now and

__ gin __ ning is now __ and ever fhall be and ever fhall be

__ gin __ ning is __ __ __ now __ __ is __ __ now __ __ and ever fhall

with - out end and e-ver shall be -

ever shall be world with - out end and

world - - - without end and ever shall be world with - out - -

be world without end world - - with - - out - - - -

6 5 3 4 2 6 5 6

world - - without - - - end A - - -

e-ver shall be - - world without - - - end A - - -

end - - - A - - - - men - - - A -

end - - - A - - - men - - - A - -

3 6 5 6

men - - A - - - - - - - men.

men - - A - - - - - - men.

- - - - men A - - - - - - men.

- - - men - A - - - - - - men.

men - A - - - - - men.

6 6 6 4 3

ANTHEM.
For two Sopranos and a Bass.

Revelations Chapter the 19th.

Dr. Blow.

Moderato.

Organ.

And I heard a great

I was in the Spi___rit on the Lords Day

Voice of much people in Heav'n___ say_____ing

And I

heard a great Voice of much people in Heav'n___ say_____

This Anthem was Originally Composed for Four Voices but Arranged for Three by the Editor.

And I heard a great Voice of much people in Heav'n fay - - - - -
- - ing
Hal - le -
6
4
6
5
Hal - le - lu - jah Hal - le - - - lu - - jah Hal - le - lu - - -
- - ing
And I
- - lu - - jah Hal - - le - - lu - - jah
Hal - - le - - lu - - -
6
6
6
6
4
5
- jah
Hal - le -
heard a great Voice of much peo-ple in Heav'n fay - - - - - - - ing
- - jah
6
8 7

_ lu _ _jah Hal _le _ _ lu _ _ _jah Hal _ le _ _lu _ _ jah Hal _ _ le _ _

Hal _ le _ _lu _ _jah Hal _ _ le _ _ lu _ _jah Hal _le _ _lu _ _jah Hal _

Hal _ _le _ _ lu _ _ jah Hal _ _ le _ _ lu _ _ jah Hal _ _le _ _lu _ _jah

6 5 6 6 6 4
5 3

Organ.

_ lu _ _ _ jah

_ le _ lu _ _ _jah

Hal _le _ _lu _ _ jah

4 7

Hal _ _le _ _lu _ _jah   Sal _ va _tion and glo _ ry and

Sal _ va _tion and glo _ ry and honour and Pow'r and

Sal _ va _tion and glo _ ry and honour and

7

honour and pow'r un — to the Lord our God un — to — the Lord our God Sal —

honour and pow'r un — to the Lord our God un — to — the Lord our God

pow'r and pow'r un — to the Lord our God un — to the Lord our God Sal —

— — vation and Glory and honour and pow'r and pow'r un — to — the Lord our God un —

Sal — vation and Glory and honour and pow'r un — to — the Lord our God un —

— — vation and Glory and honour and pow'r and pow'r un — to — the Lord our God un —

— to — the Lord our God

— to — the Lord our God

— to — the Lord our God

For

And a
true and righteous are his Judgments and again they faid Hal - le - - - lu - - jah Hal - - -
And a
-gain they faid Halle - - lu - - jah Hal - le - - lu - - jah Halle - lu - - jah again they faid
- - - - - - le - - lu - - jah - - - - Hal - - le Hal - - le - - lu - - jah
-gain they faid Halle - - lu - - jah Hal - le - - lu - - jah Halle - lu - - jah again they faid
pia.
Hal - le - lu - - jah - - - - Hal - le - lu - jah
Organ.
again they faid Hal - le - lu - jah
Halle - - lu - - jah again they faid Halle - - lu - - jah

Recit: Bass.
And the four and twenty Elders and the four Beasts fell down fell down and worship-
-ed God that sat on the Throne say-ing A-
Moderato.
And again they said Hal-le-
And again they said Hal-le-lu-jah Hal-le-lu-
-men
And again they said Hal-le-
Moderato.
-lu-jah Hal-le-lu-jah Halle-lu-jah again they said Hal-le-lu-
-jah Hal-le Hal-le-lu-jah
-lu-jah Hal-le-lu-jah Hal-le-lu-jah again they said Hal-le-lu-

_jah ___ _ _ _ _ Hal_le_lu_ _jah

again they said Hal_le_lu _ jah

_ _jah again they said Halle_lu _ _ jah

6   6 7   6 5
        4 3

And a Voice came out of the Throne say_ _ _ _ _ ing

Praise our

6   6 7 6   7 6 6

Praise our God   And ye that

Praise our God _ _ _ all _ _ ye his Servants all ye his Servants

God   Praise our God   all _ _   all _ _ all ye his Servants

6   7 6   7 6   6

fear him that fear him And ye that fear him both fmall and great that fear him both
pia.
And ye that fear him And ye that fear him both fmall and great that fear him both
pia.
And ye that fear him that fear him both fmall and great that fear him both
ppia.
Organ.
fmall and great that fear him both fmall and great
ppia.
fmall and great that fear him both fmall and great
ppia.
fmall and great that fear him both fmall and great
ppia.
And I heard as it were as it were the Voice of a great

multitude of a great mul_titude of ma_ _ny
of a great mul_titude of ma_ny
of a great mul_titude And as the Voice of ma_ _ny waters of ma_ _ny
wa_ters And as the Voice of migh_ _ty Thundriugs of migh_ _ty Thundrings
wa_ters of mighty Thundrings
wa_ters of mighty Thundrings
Hal_ _le_ _ _lu_ _jah
Hal_ _le_ _ _lu_ _ _jah
fay_ _ing Hal_ _le_ _ _lu_ _jah Hal_ _le_ _ _lu_ _ _jah

Slow.

Hal__le__ __lu__ __jah Hal__le__lu__ __jah Hal__le__lu__jah Hal__le__

Hal__le__ __lu__ __jah Hal__le__lu__ __jah Hal__le__lu__jah Hal__le__

Hal__le__ __lu__jah Hal__le__ __lu__ __jah Hal__le__ __lu__jah Hal__le__

Slow.

6

__lujah Organ.

__lujah

__lujah

Recit: Bass.

For the Lord God Omnipotent reigneth the Lord God Omnipotent reign__ __eth

6   7 6   4   6 5b   6 7
                    2   4 3

Chearful.

Let us be glad and rejoice and give ho__ __nour to him

Let us be glad and rejoice and rejoice and give ho__ __nour to him

Let us be glad and rejoice and rejoice and give honour to him for the Marriage of the

Chearful.   6   7 6   7 6   6   #6   pia. 6   6

32

Slow.
pia.
Hal_ _le_ _ _lu_ _ _jah Hal_ _ _le_ _lu_ _ _jah Hal_ _ _le_ _
Slow.
pia.
Hal_ _le_ _ _lu_ _ _ _jah Hal_ _le_ _lu_ _ _ _jah Hal_ _ _le_ _
Slow.
pia.
Hal_ _ _le_ _ _lu_ _ _jah Hal_ _le_ _ _ _lu_ _ _ _jah Hal_ _ _le_ _
Slow.
pia.
_ _lu_ _jah_ Hal_ _le_ _lu_ _jah Hal_ _le_ _ _lu_ _ _jah Hal_ _le_ _
ppia.
_ _lu_ _jah Hal_ _le_ _lu_ _jah Hal_ _le_ _ _lu_ _ _ _jah Hal_ _le_ _
ppia.
_ _lu_ _jah Hal_ _le_ _lu_ _jah Hal_ _le_ _ _lu_ _jah Hal_ _le_ _ _
ppia.
6
_ _lu_ _ _jah Hal_ _le_ _lu_ _jah_ Hal_ _le_ _lu_ _jah
tr
_ _lu_ _ _jah Hal_ _le_ _lu_ _jah Hal_ _le_ _ _lu_ _jah
tr
_ _lu_ _ _jah Hal_ _le_ _lu_ _jah Hal_ _le_ _lu_ _jah
6
6

SOLO ANTHEM.
For a Soprano.

Psalm 89th.   Purcell.

Organ.

Moderato.   pia.   My Song shall be alway of the

lo — ving kindness of the Lord   My Song shall be alway of the

lo — — — ving kindness of the Lord   with my Mouth will I

ever be shewing forth thy truth   with my Mouth will I — ever be

shewing forth thy truth from one ge — ne — ra — —

— tion to a — no — — ther —

This Anthem may be Sung by a Tenor.

Recit: flow.

O Lord   O Lord the very Heav'ns shall praise thy Won _ _ _ _

_ _ drous works   O _ _ _ Lord the very Heav'ns shall praise thy won _ _

_ _ _ drous works and thy truth in the Congrega_tion of the Saints

and thy truth in the Congre-gation of the Saints. Mod.to

For who is he among the Clouds that shall be compar'd unto the Lord

For who is he among the Clouds that shall be compar'd un _ _to the

Lord _ _ for who is he For who is he among the Clouds that shall be com_

-par'd unto the Lord And what is he what what is He is he a-mong the

Gods that shall be like un_to the Lord and what is he

what what is he among the Gods that shall be like un_to the

Lord what what what is he among the Gods that shall be like that shall be

like un__to the Lord what what what is he a-mong the

Gods that shall be like that shall be like un_to the Lord

Recit:

God is very great - - ly to be fear'd in the council of the Saints and to be had in Re-

- verence of all them that are round - - - - a - - bout Him   God

is very greatly is very greatly to be fear'd and to be had in Re - verence of all

them that are round - - - - - - - - are round   about Him

Recit: flow.

O - - - - Lord God of Hosts, who,   who is 'ke un -to- Thee?

O - - - - - Lord   God - of Hosts, who, who, who is like unto - Thee?

Largo Andante.

Thy truth most   migh - - - - ty Lord is on ev - -ry side thy truth most migh _ _ _ ty Lord moſt migh _ _ _ _ _ _ _ _ _ _ _ _ ty

Lord is on ev _ _ ry Side. Thou ru _ leſt the

ra _ _ _ _ _ ging of the Sea Thou ruleſt the ra _ _ _ _ _

_ _ ging of the Sea

Thou ſtilleſt the waves thereof when they a _ riſe _ _ _ _ _ _ _

_ _ Thou ſtilleſt the waves thereof Thou ſtilleſt the waves thereof when they a _ riſe _ _

Thou ftilleft the waves thereof Thou ftilleft the waves there _

_ of the waves _ _ _ _ _ thereof when they _ a _ rife

Largo Maestoso.

Thou haft a Migh _ _ ty migh _ ty migh _ ty arm thou

haft a migh _ ty migh _ ty migh _ ty arm ftrong is thy hand ftrong is thy

hand and high, and high _ _ is thy right _ _ _ hand _ _

Thou hast a Migh--ty migh - - ty Arm strong is thy hand
pia.
for.
for.
strong is thy hand and high and high - - - - - is thy right hand
pia.
for.
pia.
ppia.
Righteousnefs and Equity are the Ha --bi _tation of thy Seat Righteousnefs, and
pia.
ppia.
Equity are the Ha-- bi-- ta - - - - - - - - - - - - - tion of Thy Seat.
tr.
Recit: flow.
Mercy and Truth fhall go before Thy face Mercy and Truth Mercy and
truth fhall go before Thy face
tr.
Organ Chords
pia.
Vivace
Halle--lu - - - - jah
Organ.
for.
pia.
for.

Hal le lu — jah Hal — — le lu —

— jah Hal — le — lu — — — jah Hal le —

— lu — — jah Hal-le-lu — — jah

Hal — — — — — — le-lu — jah —

— Hal — le — lu — jah Hal — — —

— le-lu — jah Hal — — — le-lu — jah.

ANTHEM.
For two Sopranos.

Dr. Green.

Largo.

Blessed are those that are undefilled in the way and walk in the Law of the Lord and walk in the Law of the Lord in the Law in the Law of the Lord Blessed are

Blessed are those that are undefilled in the way and walk in the Law of the Lord in the Law of the Lord in the Law of the Lord

they - - that keep his Tes - - ti - mo - nies and feek him with their
Blefsed are they that keep - his Tes - ti - monies and feek - - him with their
Organ.
- - whole heart Blefsed are they that keep his Tes - - ti -
whole heart Blefsed are they that keep that keep his Tes - - ti - -
for.
pia.
- - monies and feek - - him with their whole - heart and feek - - him
- - monies and feek him with - their whole - heart and - feek - -
Organ.
with their whole Heart.
- - him with their whole Heart
for.

Solo First Soprano.
Recit:
Thou hast Charged that we shall diligently keep thy Commandments
Thou hast charged that we shall di_ligently keep thy Commandments
Andante.
Organ.
O that my ways were made so _ direct that I might keep that I might
keep thy Statutes O that my ways were made so _ di_ _rect that I might
keep that I might keep thy Statutes o_ _pen Thou mine Eyes o_ _pen Thou mine
Eyes that I may see the won_ _ drous things the wondrous things of Thy _

Law O that my ways were made so direct that I might keep that I might

keep thy Statutes o_pen Thou mine eyes o_pen Thou mine eyes that I may

see the won _ _ _ _ drous things of Thy Law o_pen thou mine

eyes o_pen Thou mine eyes that I may see the won _ _ _ _

_ _ _ _ _ drous things of Thy _ law that I may see that I may

see the won _ _ _ _ drous the wondrous things of thy _ law

DUETTO.

Organ.

Vivace.

Then will I talk will I talk of thy Commandments and have respect un _

Vivace.

_ to _ _ thy ways   Then will I   talk will I talk of thy Com _

Then will I   talk will I   talk of thy Commandments and have   res _

_ mandments and have res _ _ pect un _ _ _ to _ _ thy   ways

_ _ pect   and have res _ _ pect   un _ _ to   thy   ways   Then will I

Then will I   talk of thy Commandments and   have   res _ _ pect   un _

talk of thy Commandments and   have   res _ _ 'pect   and have   res _ _ pect un _ _ to thy ways and have respect un _ to _ thy ways

_ _to thy ways and have respect un to thy ways   My de_

my delight shall be in thy Sta__tutes

light shall be in thy _ Sta_tutes   my delight shall be in thy

my_ _ delight shall be shall be in thy Statutes and I will not I will not for_

_ _ _ Sta_tutes thy Sta _ _ _ _ _ tutes   I will not for_

_ _get _ thy word   I will not for_get _ thy word

_ _ get _ thy word and I will not I will not for_get _ thy word Then will I

Then will I talk will I talk of thy Commandments and have res_ _

talk will I talk of thy Commandments and have res_ _ pect and have res_ _

_ _pect un_ _to thy ways and have res_ pect un_ _to_ _ thy

_ _pect un_ _to thy ways and have res_ pect un_ _to thy

ways My_ _ delight fhall be in thy_ _ Sta_ _tutes

ways My_ _ de_light fhall

My_ _ de_light fhall be my de_light fhall be fhall

be in thy_ _ Sta_ _tutes my de_light fhall be my de_light fhall be in thy Sta___tutes shall be in___thy___Sta___

be in thy Sta___tutes shall be in thy Sta___

___tutes and I will not I will not for___get___thy word I

___tutes I will not for___get___thy word and I will not I

will not for_get___thy word I will not I will not forget___thy

will not for-get___thy word I will not forget___thy

Organ.

word.

word.

TRIO.

For two Sopranos and a Bass.

Psalm 49th   Steffani.

pia.
_ ther high and low rich and poor ponder it with your Ears all ye that
pia.
O hear ye this high and low rich and poor ponder
pia.
ponder it with your Ears all ye that dwell in the Land O
pia.
dwell in the land High and low rich and poor high and
for.
it with your Ears all ye that dwell in the Land High and low rich and poor one with a _
for.
hear ye this all ye peo _ ple O hear ye this ponder
for.
low rich and poor one with a _ _ no _ _ _ _ _ _ ther
_ _ no _ _ _ _ _ ther high and low rich and poor one with a _ no _ _ _ _
it with your Ears all ye that dwell in the land High and low rich and

pon_der it with your Ears all ye that dwell in the land High and

_ther O hear ye this all ye peo__ple O

poor one with a __ no ____ ther ponder it with your Ears all ye

low rich and poor one with a __ no ___ ther O hear ye this

hear ye this ponder it with your

peo _ ple High and low rich and poor one with a _ no ___

all ye peo __ ple O hear ye this

Ears all ye that dwell in the land high and low rich and poor one with a _

_ther ponder it with your Ears all ye that dwell in the land high and

Largo.
Cres.
fr. Tempo
high and low rich and poor one with a - - - no - - - - ther God is
no - - - - - - ther one with a - - - no - - - ther God is
low rich and poor rich and poor one with a - no - - - - ther God is
our God our God for ev_er and e - - - - ver for God is
our God our God for ev_er and e - - - - ver for God is
our God our God for ev_er and e - - - - ver for God is
our God our God for ever and e - - - - ver
our God our God for ever and e - - - - ver
our God our God for ever and e - - - - ver

ANTHEM.

For a Soprano.

Psalm 15th.   Marcello.

Lord who shall dwell in thy Ta—bernacle in thy Ta—ber—nacle who shall dwell in thy Tabernacle or rest up—on thy holy mountain who shall dwell in thy——taber—na—cle Lord who shall dwell in thy taber———na———cle or rest up-on thy holy moun—tain

dwell in thy Tabernacle or rest upon thy holy mountain who shall dwell in thy taber — na —

— cle or rest upon thy holy mountain who shall rest — — — up —

— on thy holy moun — — tain

Organ.

Lento.   He   He

He   even   he that walketh upright — ly   even he that walketh up —

— rightly walketh upright — ly and worketh righteousness and worketh righteousness

Yea even He that walketh up-rightly walketh upright-ly and worketh righteousfs

- and ever spea-keth the truth the truth fpeaketh the truth - from his

Heart

Organ.

Vivace.

for.

He that doeth thefe things fhall

ne-ver be mo - - ved He that doeth thefe things fhall never be moved shall ne — — ver be mo — — ved He that doeth these

things He that doeth these things shall ne—ver be mo — — —

— — ved He that doeth these things shall never be moved shall ne — —

— — ver be mo — — — ved He that doeth these things

He that doeth these things He that doeth these things shall ne—ver be

mo — — ved He that doeth these things He that

Organ.
doeth these things shall - - not - - be - - mo - - -
for.
pia.
- ved He that doeth these things Organ. shall - - not - - be - -
for.
Organ.
mo - - - ved shall ne - ver be mo - - - ved He that doeth these
for.
pia
Organ.
things shall never be moved shall ne - - - ver be mo - - - - ved
for.
He that doeth these things these things shall never be moved shall ne - - -
pia.
- - - ver be mo - - - ved
for.

ANTHEM.

For an Alto and Bass.

Psalm 133ᵈ. Dʳ Nares.

Organ. Vivace.

Behold Behold Behold how good and Joy-ful a thing — it is Bre-

_thren to dwell to ge-ther in U-ni-ty

Behold Behold Behold how good and Joy-ful a thing — it is

Joy-ful a thing — it is Bre-thren to dwell to ge-ther in U-ni-ty

Be-

Behold Behold _ how good and joy _ ful a thing it is how Joy _ _ _ _
_ hold Behold Behold how good and joy _ ful a thing it is how Joy _ _ _ _
_ _ _ _ _ _ _ ful a thing it is _ how Joy _ _ _ _ _ _ _ _ _
_ _ _ _ _ _ _ ful a thing it is how Joy _ _ _ _ _ _ _ _ _
_ ful a thing it is _ Bre _ thren to dwell to _ gether in U _ ni _ ty Behold _ _
_ _ ful a thing it is _ Bre _ thren to dwell to _ gether in U _ ni _ ty Behold _ _ Be _ _
_ how good and joy _ ful a thing it is Behold how good and Joy _ ful
_ hold how good and joy _ ful a thing it is Behold how good and

how good and Joy—ful ... how Joy—ful how Joy—ful a thing it

Joy—ful ... how good and Joy—ful how Joy—ful how Joy—ful a thing it.

is Bre—thren to dwell to—ge—ther in U——ni—ty Behold how good and

is to dwell—— to—ge—ther in U——ni—ty Behold how good and

Joy—ful a thing it is to dwell to—ge—ther in U——ni—ty

Joy—ful a thing it is to dwell to—ge—ther in U——ni—

—ty to dwell to—ge—ther in U——ni—ty Be—hold how

—ty to dwell to—ge—ther in U——ni—ty Be—hold how

good and joyful it is Bre_thren to dwell to_ge_ther in U_ni_ty Brethren to dwell to_

good and joyful it is Bre_thren to dwell to_ge_ther in U_ni_ty Brethren to dwell to_

_ge__ther in U_ni__ty.   Organ.

_ge__ther in U_ni__ty.

Solo Bass.

Andante Vivace.

for.

Tasto Solo.   Organ.   Tasto Solo.

It is like the dew of Hermon which fell upon the hill of

Tasto Solo.

Sion   for there the Lord   promised His   Blessing   and life _ for ever _ more for ever more and life _ _ _ for ever _ more

It is like the dew of Hermon which fell upon the hill of

Si _ on which fell upon the Hill of Si _ on For there the Lord

promifed His blefsing and life for evermore for e _ _ ver _ more and

life for evermore for e _ _ vermore

Vivace. Behold how good and Joy _ ful a thing _ it is to dwell to _

Vivace. Behold how good and Joy _ ful a thing _ it is to dwell to _

-gether in U _ _nity to dwell together in U _ _ _ ni _ _ty Behold how

-gether in U _ _ni _ ty to dwell to _ gether in U _ _ _ ni _ ty Behold how

good and joyful it is Brethren to dwell to _ ge _ ther in U _ _ ni _ ty Brethren to dwell to.

good and joyful it is Brethren to dwell to _ ge _ ther in U _ _ ni _ ty Brethren to dwell to.

-ge _ _ ther in U _ _ ni _ _ ty Organ.

-ge _ _ther in U _ _ ni _ _ ty

Largo. Solo alto.

Peace be with _ in thy walls Peace be with _ in thy _ _ walls and

plenteousness within thy pa _ la _ ces and plenteousness within thy Palaces

Peace be with_in thy _ walls   Peace be with_in_ _ thy

walls   and plenteousnefs within thy Palaces   plenteousnefs within thy Palaces

Peace be with_in thy _ _ walls   Peace be with_in   thy   walls

Vivace. For my Brethren   and Companions fake I will   wifh   will wifh I will

Vivace. For my Brethren   and Companions fake   I will wifh   will

with thee Profpe_ri_ty   For my Bre_thren and Companions

with thee Profperi_ty   For my Bre-thren and Companions fake I will

sake I will wish will wish thee Prospe _ _ ri _ ty for my Brethren and Companions

wish will wish will wish thee Prospe _ _ ri _ ty for my Brethren and Companions

4 3 6 6 5 7 7 6 6 # for. 4 6
        4 # # #   4   2

sake I will wish will wish thee Pros pe _ _ ri _ ty I will wish thee Prosperi _ ty will

sake I will wish will wish thee Prospe _ ri _ ty I will wish thee Prosperi _ ty will

6 5 6 _ 4 3 6 5 6 # 7 6 5
4 3 5   4 # 4 #   4 #

wish thee Prospe _ ri _ ty will wish will wish I will wish thee Pros _ pe _ _ ri _

wish thee Prospe _ ri _ ty will wish I will wish I will wish thee Pros _ pe _ _ ri _

7 6 5 # b7 b7 6 5   6 5 6 5
5 4 3 3   4 3   4 3 4 3

_ ty I will wish will wish I will wish thee Pros _ pe _ ri _ ty

_ _ ty I will wish I will wish I will wish thee Pros _ pe _ _ ri _ ty

b7 6 5   6 5 6 5
   4 3   4 3 4 3

DUETTO.
For a Soprano & Tenor.

Psalm 51st Verse 2nd.   Handel.

Largo Andante.

Wash me throughly from my — Wickedness from my — Wickedness and cleanse me cleanse me from my — Sin — — from my — Sin

Wash me throughly from my — Wickedness from my —

Wash me throughly

wickednefs and cleanse me   cleanse me from my __ Sin __ __ __

Wash me   throughly   from my_   wick-ednefs   from my __ wickednefs and

from my __ Sin   Wash me   throughly   from my   wicked-nefs

from my _ : Sin   Wash me   throughly from my _ wickednefs and

Wash me   throughly   from my_ wicked-nefs from my   wickednefs and

cleanfe me from my   Sin   *Organ.*   Wash me

cleanfe me from my   Sin.

throughly   wash me   throughly   wash me   throughly   wash me

Wash me throughly   wash me   throughly   wash me   throughly

throughly   wash me ___ throughly from my ___ wick-ednefs

wash me   throughly   wash me ___ throughly from my ___ wick-ednefs

from my ___ wick-ednefs and cleanse me from my Sin

from my ___ wick-ednefs and cleanse me from my Sin

wash me   through-ly   wash me

wash me   throughly from   my   wick-ednefs and cleanse ___ me from my

pia.
for.
throughly
wash me throughly
from my wicked_nefs
sin_ _ _ from my_ _ sin _ _ _ _ _ _ _ _ _ _ _ _ _ _ _
Cres:
pia.
Cres:
for.
wash me througho_ly from my _ wick_ednefs from my wick_ednefs &
pia.
_ _ _ _ _ wash me through_ly from my _ wick_ed_ _nefs and cleanse
Cres.
fo:
Organ.
tr
cleanse me from my sin_ _ _ _
me_from my sin_ _ _ _ _
for.
tr

ANTHEM.

For three Voices.

Alto, Tenor and Bass.

Psalm. 9.th   Dr. Croft.

Organ..   Moderato.

I will give thanks   will give thanks _ _ _ _ _

An Octave lower.   I will give thanks   will give thanks _ _ _

pia.

un _ _to Thee O _ _ Lord

un _ _to Thee O _ _ Lord

I will give thanks will give thanks _ _

I will give thanks

untoThee O Lord

I will give thanks _ _ _ _ _ give thanks give

_ _ will give thanks _ _ _ _ give thanks give

will give thanks _ _ _ give thanks _ _

thanks give thanks _ _ _ _ give thanks _ _

thanks give thanks give thanks _ _ _ _ _ _

_ _ give thanks _ _ _ I will give

un__to Thee I will give thanks unto Thee O Lord give

un__to Thee I will give thanks un_to Thee O Lord I

thanks un__to Thee I will give thanks un_to Thee O Lord I

thanks

will give thanks I will give thanks

will give thanks I will give thanks

unto Thee O _ _ Lord with my whole _ _ heart

with my whole heart

unto Thee O _ _ Lord with my whole _ _ heart

Vivace. I will speak of all all all

I will speak of all all all Thy mar — — — — —

Vivace. I will speak of all all all Thy mar — — — —

6   6   6   6

Thy mar — — — — — — ve — lous marve — lous works

— — ve — lous works Thy mar — — — — — ve — lous

— — ve — lous works Thy mar — ve — lous works

6   6 / 5   6   6 / 5 #

I will speak of all all all

marve — — lous works will speak of all Thy mar — — — — —

I will speak of all all all will speak of all all

6 / 4   #   #   6   6 / 4   6   6   b

will ſpeak of all all all Thy mar- - ve - lous marve - lous
- - ve - lous works all all all all Thy marve - lous marve - - lous
I will ſpeak of all all all Thy marvelous works will ſpeak of
works I will ſpeak of all all all all
works will ſpeak of all all all all all all
all I will ſpeak of all all all all all
all Thy mar - - - - - - - ve - lous
all Thy mar - - velous works all thy mar - - - - - ve - lous
all all Thy mar - - - - - - - - ve - lous

marve_lous works all all   all   all Thy

mar_ve_lous works all all   all   all Thy mar_ velous

mar_ve_lous works   all all   all   all Thy mar ___

6 3   b   6b   6 3
4   4b

Organ tacet.

mar ___ ___ ___ ___ ___ ___ ve_lous marve_lous works.

works all Thy mar ___ ___ ___ ___ ve_lous marve_lous works.

___ ___ ___ ___ ___ ___ ve_lous marve_lous works.

6   6   7   6   6 3
4

Solo Alto.

Moderato.

I will be glad and re joice _ _ _ _ _ _ _ in Thee

Organ.

will be glad _ _ _

_ _ _ will be glad _ _ _ _ and re _ joice _ rejoice _ re_

_joice _ in Thee

Yea my fongs will I_

make of Thy Name O _ _ O _ _ O _ _

_ O _ _ _ _ Thou moft high _ _ eft O Thou moft higheft

Yea my fongs will I make _ _ O _ _ _ _ _ _ _

- - Thou most high - est O Thou most high - est
Yea my songs will I make of thy
Name O - - - O - - - Thou most high - - - est
O Thou most highest

Solo Bass.

Moderato.

For Thou haft maintain—ed maintain — — — — —

— — ed my right and my caufe

For Thou haft maintain—ed maintain — — —

— — ed my right   my

right and my   cause   Thou art

fet in the Throne Thou art fet in the Throne - - that
for. pia.
jud - gest right art fet in the Throne that jud - - gest
for. pia.
Organ pia.
right For Thou hast main -
for. pia.
- tained my right and my cause Thou art fet in the Throne art
for. pia.
fet in the Throne the Throne - - that jud - gest right
Organ. pia.
for.

Largo. Moderato.

O   O   O praise the Lord   Shew the people of his doings shew the

O   O   O praise the Lord   Shew the people of his doings

O   O   O praise the Lord   Shew the people of his doings   the

Largo. Moderato.

people the   peo-ple   of   his   doings shew the   peo-ple   of   his

Shew the people   of   his doings shew the   peo-ple   of   his

people the   peo-ple   of   his   doings shew the   peo-ple   of   his

doings shew the people   the   people   of   his   do-ings

doings   shew the people   of   his   do-ings

doings   the people   the   people   of   his   do-ings

SOLO.
For a Soprano.

Psalm 99th Verse 9th.

Handel.

This Solo may be Sung by a Tenor.

O magni_fy _ _ _ _ _ _ the Lord O magni_fy the Lord and

wor_ _fhip him and wor_ _fhip him up_on his ho_ _ _ly

Hill upon his holy Hill_ _ upon his holy Hill_ _ and wor_ _fhip

him up_ on his holy Hill

For _ _ the Lord _ our God _ is Holy

For _ _ the Lord _ our God is holy _ is ho _ _ _ _ _ ly _ the

Lord our God is ho _ _ ly is ho _ _ _ ly the Lord our God is

ho _ _ ly is ho _ _ _ ly

O magni _ _

for.
pia.
fy the Lord O mag-ni-fy the Lord O magni-fy
the Lord O mag-ni-fy the Lord and wor-ship him and wor-ship him upon his ho-ly Hill upon his holy Hill and wor-ship Him upon his Ho-ly Hill

DUETTO.
For two Tenors.

C. Marcello.

O hold Thou — me up guide me in — the path guide me in

O hold Thou — me up guide me in —

— the path of Thy Commandments I am Thy servant teach me Thy

— — the path of Thy Commandments I am Thy servant teach me Thy

statutes hold up my goings my go — — ings in

statutes hold up my goings my go — — — — — ings my goings in

This Duetto may be Sung by two Sopranos.

all thy paths fo that my footfteps may not be
all thy paths may not be moved may not be
moved O hold Thou up - - my - - - go - - - ings
moved fo that my footfteps may not be moved O hold Thou
fo that my footfteps may not be moved fo that my footfteps may not be mo -
up - - my - - go - - - ings fo that my footfteps may not be mo -
- ved. So that my footfteps may not be mo - ved.
- ved. So that my footfteps may not be mo - ved.

I call up _ _ _ on Thee In time of _ _ trou _
I call up _ _ _ on
_ _ ble I call up _ _ _ on Thee for Thou wilt hear me Thou art my
Thee in time of _ _ trou _ _ ble for Thou wilt hear me Thou art my
refuge lead me and guide me I call up _ on Thee up _ _
refuge lead me and guide me I call up _ on Thee I call _ _ _ up _ _
_ _ on _ _ _ Thee for Thou wilt hear me give Ear un _ to me
_ _ on Thee O Lord for Thou wilt hear me hafte Thee to

for.
give Ear un_to me haste Thee to help me I call up_on_ _
for.
help me give Ear un_to me haste Thee to help me give Ear un_
for.
pia.
Thee_ _ O_ _ Lord give Ear un_to me haste Thee to
pia.
_to me haste Thee to help me I call up_on_ Thee_ _ O_
pia.
ppia.
for.
help me O hearken hearken un_to_my_words O hearken hearken un_
ppia.
for.
Lord O hearken hearken un_to_my_words O hearken hearken un_
ppia.
for.
_to_my_words.
Organ.
_to_my_words.

DUETTO.

For two Sopranos.

Psalm 34th verse the 3d.

Steffani.

Moderato.

O praise the Lord _ with me and let us mag _ ni _ fy his
name and let us mag _ ni _ fy his name O praise the Lord _ _ with
me and let us mag _ ni _ fy his Name

O praise the Lord _ _ with
me and let us mag _ ni _ fy his name O praise the Lord _ _ _ with
me and let us mag _ ni _ fy his name and let us mag _ ni _ fy his

This Duetto may be Sung by two Tenors.

O praise the Lord _ _ _ with me and let us mag _ ni _ fy his

name and let us mag _ ni _ fy his name O praise the Lord _ _ _ with

name O praise the Lord _ _ _ _ with me and let us mag _ ni _ fy his

me and let us mag _ ni _ fy his name and let us mag _ ni _ fy his

Name

and let us mag _ ni _ fy his

Name

name let us mag _ ni _ fy his name mag _ _ _ ni _ _ _ fy

let us mag _ ni _ fy his name let us magni _ fy his

for.
- - his name to - - ge - ther let us magni - fy his name let us magni - fy his
name to - - - ge - - ther
let us magni - fy his
name mag - ni - fy - - his name to ge - - ther
pia.
name mag - ni - fy his name his name to - - ge - - ther O praise the Lord with
me and let us magni - fy his name - to - - - ge - - ther
and let us
magni - fy his name and let us mag - ni - fy his name mag - - - ni - fy
and let us magni - fy his name mag - - - ni - fy his

pia.
his name to - ge - - ther mag - ni - fy - - mag - - ni - fy - -
pia.
name his name to - - ge - - - - ther mag - - ni - - fy - -
pia.
for.
- - his name to - - ge - - ther and magni - - fy his name his name to - -
for.
- - his name to - - - ge - - - - ther and magni - fy his name to - -
for.
Organ.
- - ge - - - - ther
- - - - ge - - - - ther

SOLO ANTHEM.
For a Soprano.

Psalm 13th.   Clarke.

Largo Andante. How long wilt Thou for‑get me

How long wilt Thou for‑get me   O Lord wilt Thou for‑

‑get me for ever   How — long   How — long wilt Thou hide Thy face

from me   How — long   O — — Lord wilt thou hide Thy face from me

How long shall I seek counsel in my   Soul   And be fo

This Anthem may be Sung by a Tenor.

vex——ed in my heart How long how long shall I seek

Counsel in my Soul and be so vex——ed and be so vexed in my heart

Organ.

How long shall mine

e——nemies tri——umph o——ver me How——long How——

long How long shall mine e——nemies tri——umph o——ver me Consider and

Organ.

hear me O Lord my God Consider Consider Con—

...fider and hear me O Lord my God lighten mine Eyes lighten mine Eyes that I

fleep not in death that I fleep _ _ _ not fleep not in death lighten mine Eyes that I

fleep not in death that I fleep _ _ not I fleep _ _ not fleep not in Death that I

fleep _ _ _ not I fleep _ _ _ not fleep not in Death

Recit: Slow.

Left mine e-nemy fay I have prevail'd againft him Left mine e-nemy

fay I have prevail'd againft him For if I be caft down they that trouble me they that trouble me

will rejoice at it they that trouble me they that trouble me will re-joice at it
Organ.
Andante.
for.
But my truft is in thy
pia.
mer-cy and my heart is joyful my heart is joy-ful in thy fal-
-vation my heart is Joyful in Thy fal-vation is joy
for.
ful in thy fal-vation is joy
pia.
ful in thy fal-va-tion

TRIO.

For an Alto Tenor & Bass.

Psalm the 18th.   Marcello.

Organ.

Grave.

I will al_ _way love_ _Thee_ _O Lord_ _O Lord my

strength O Lord_ _O Lord_ _ _my strength_ _I will

Tenor an Octave lower.

O Lord my strength O_ Lord my strength I will alway love_

O Lord my strength O Lord my strength   I will

love - - - will al_way love thee For thou art - - my
- - I will al_way love - - - thee
love will al_way love - - - thee
6 5 6 7
Organ.
fto_ny rock and houfe - - of my - - de - - fence my For-
5 3 6 6 6 5 6
-trefs my For--trefs and my de-li--ver--er For thou art - - my
For thou art - - my
For thou art - - my
6 5 5 3 6 4 7 5 5 3 6 6

Organ.
ſto_ny rock, and houſe_ _ of my_ _ de_ _ _fence my For_ _
ſto_ny rock, and houſe_ _ of my_ _ de_ _ _fence my For_ _
ſto_ny rock, and houſe_ _ of my_ _ de_ _ _fence my For_ _
_ _treſs my For_ _treſs and my de_ _li_ _verer
_ _treſs my For_ _treſs and my de_ _li_ _verer
_ _treſs my For_ _treſs and my de_ _li_ _verer my Sa_ _ _ _ _ _viour my
my Sa_ _ _
God and my might_ _ in whom I_ _ _ truſt my Saviour my

- - viour - - my God - and my might - - in whom I - - truſt
Sa - - viour my God and my might my might in whom I truſt
Organ.
my Buck - - ler - - the Horn al - ſo of my - - Sal - - va - - - -
my Buck - - ler - - the Horn al - ſo of my - - Sal - - va - - - -
my Buck - - ler - - the Horn al - ſo of my - - Sal - - va - - -
Organ.
- - tion my Re - - fuge my Re - - fuge and my ſtrong Tow'r.
- - tion my Re - - fuge my Re - - fuge and my ſtrong Tow'r.
- - tion my Re - - fuge my Re - - fuge and my ſtrong Tow'r.